Tertullian

The Chaplet or De Corona

Tertullian

The Chaplet or De Corona

Tertullian
The Chaplet or De Corona

Published by
Lighthouse Christian Publishing
SAN 257-4330
5531 Dufferin Drive
Savage, Minnesota, 55378
United States of America

www.lighthousechristianpublishing.com

Tertullian

Introductory Note.

[a.d. 145–220.] When our Lord repulsed the woman of Canaan (Matt. xv. 22) with apparent harshness, he applied to her people the epithet *dogs*, with which the children of Israel had thought it piety to reproach them. When He accepted her faith and caused it to be recorded for our learning, He did something more: He reversed the curse of the Canaanite and showed that the Church was designed "for all people;" Catholic alike for all time and for all sorts and conditions of men.

Thus the North-African Church was loved before it was born: the Good Shepherd was gently leading those "that were with young." Here was the charter of those Christians to be a Church, who then were Canaanites in the land of their father Ham. It is remarkable indeed that among these pilgrims and strangers to the West the first elements of Latin Christianity come into view. Even at the close of the Second Century the Church in Rome is an inconsiderable, though prominent, member of the great confederation of Christian Churches which has its chief seats in Alexandria and Antioch, and of which the entire Literature is Greek. It is an African presbyter who takes from Latin Christendom the reproach of theological and literary barrenness and begins the great work in which, upon his foundations, Cyprian and Augustine built up, with incomparable genius, that Carthaginian School of Christian thought by which Latin Theology was dominated for centuries. It is important to note (1.) that providentially not one of these illustrious doctors died in Communion with the Roman See, pure though it was and venerable at that time; and (2.) that to the works of Augustine the Reformation in Germany and Continental Europe was largely due; while (3.) the *specialties* of the Anglican Reformation were, in like proportion, due to the writings of Tertullian and Cyprian. The hinges of great and controlling destinies for Western Europe and our own America are to be found in the period we are now approaching.

The merest school-boy knows much of the history of Carthage, and how the North Africans became Roman citizens. How they became Christians is not so clear. A melancholy destiny has enveloped Carthage from the outset, and its glory and greatness as a Christian See were transient indeed. It blazed out all at once in Tertullian, after about a century of missionary labours had been exerted upon its creation: and having given a Minucius Felix, an Arnobius and a Lactantius to adorn the earliest period of Western Ecclesiastical learning, in addition to its nobler luminaries, it rapidly declined. At the beginning of the Third Century, at a council presided over by Agrippinus, Bishop of Carthage, there were present not less than seventy bishops of the Province. A period of cruel persecutions followed, and the African Church received a baptism of blood.

Tertullian was born a heathen, and seems to have been educated at Rome, where he probably practiced as a jurisconsult. We may, perhaps, adopt most of the ideas of Allix, as conjecturally probable, and assign his birth to a.d. 145. He became a Christian about 185, and a presbyter about 190. The period of his strict orthodoxy very nearly expires with the century. He lived to an extreme old age, and some suppose even till a.d. 240. More probably we must adopt the date preferred by recent writers, a.d. 220.

It seems to be the fashion to treat of Tertullian as a Montanist, and only incidentally to celebrate his services to the Catholic Orthodoxy of Western Christendom. Were I his biographer I should reverse this course, as a mere act of justice, to say nothing of gratitude to a man of splendid intellect, to whom the filial spirit of Cyprian accorded the loving tribute of a disciple, and whose genius stamped itself upon the very words of Latin theology, and prepared the language for the labors of a Jerome. In creating the Vulgate, and so lifting the Western Churches into a position of intellectual equality with the East, the latter as well as St. Augustine himself were debtors to Tertullian in a degree not to be estimated by any other than the Providential Mind that inspired his brilliant career as a Christian.

In speaking of Tatian I laid the base for what I wished to say of Tertullian. Let God only be their judge; let us gratefully recognize the debt we owe to them. Let us read them, as we read the works of King Solomon. We must, indeed, approve of the discipline of the Primitive Age, which allowed of no compromises. The Church was struggling for existence, and could not permit any man to become her master. The more brilliant the intellect, the more dangerous to the poor Church were its perversions of her Testimony. Before the heathen tribunals, and in the market-places, it would not answer to let Christianity appear double tongued. The orthodoxy of the Church, not less than her children, was undergoing an ordeal of fire. It seems a miracle that her Testimony preserved its unity, and that heresy was branded as such by the instinct of the Faithful. Poor Tertullian was cut off by his own act. The weeping Church might bewail him as David mourned for Absalom, but like David, she could not give the Ark of God into other hands than those of the loyal and the true. I have set the writings of Tertullian in a natural and logical order, so as to aid the student, and to relieve him from the distractions of such an arrangement as one finds in Oehler's edition. Valuable as it is, the practical use of it is irritating and confusing. The reader of that edition may turn to the slightly differing schemes of Neander and Kaye, for a theoretical order of the works; but here he will find a classification which will aid his inquiries. He will find, first, those works which connect with the Apologists of the former volumes of this series: which illustrate the Church's position toward the outside world, the Jews as well as the Gentiles. Next come those works which contend with internal differences and heresies. And then, those which reflect the morals and manners of Christians. These are classed with some reference to their degrees of freedom from the Montanistic taint, and are followed, last of all, by the few tracts which belong to the melancholy period of his lapse, and are directed against the Church's orthodoxy.

Let it be borne in mind, that if this sad close of Tertullian's career cannot be extenuated, the later history of Latin Christianity forbids us to condemn him, in the tones which proceeded from the Virgin Church with authority, and which the law of her testimony and the instinct of self-preservation forced her to utter. Let us reflect that St. Bernard and after him the Schoolmen, whom we so deservedly honor, separated themselves far more absolutely than ever Tertullian did from the orthodoxy of Primitive Christendom. The schism which withdrew the West from Communion with the original seats of Christendom, and from Nicene Catholicity, was formidable beyond all expression, in comparison with Tertullian's entanglements with a delusion which the See of Rome itself had momentarily patronized. Since the Council of Trent, not a theologian of the Latins has been free from organic heresies, compared with which the fanaticism of our author was a trifling aberration. Since the late Council of the Vatican, essential Montanism has become organized in the Latin Churches: for what are the new revelations and oracles of the pontiff but the *deliria* of another claimant to the voice and inspiration of the Paraclete? Poor Tertullian! The sad influences of his decline and folly have been fatally felt in all the subsequent history of the West, but, surely subscribers to the Modern Creed of the Vatican have reason to "speak gently of *their father's* fall." To Döllinger, with the "Old Catholic" remnant only, is left the right to name the Montanists heretics, or to upbraid Tertullian as a lapser from Catholicity.

From Dr. Holmes, I append the following Introductory Notice:

(I.) Quintus Septimius Florens Tertullianus, as our author is called in the mss. of his works, is thus noticed by Jerome in his *Catalogus Scriptorum Ecclesiasticorum:* "Tertullian, a presbyter, the first Latin writer after Victor and Apollonius, was a native of the province of Africa and city of Carthage, the son of a proconsular centurion: he was a man of a sharp and vehement temper, flourished under Severus and Antoninus Caracalla, and wrote numerous works, which (as they are generally known) I think it unnecessary to particularize. I saw at Concordia, in Italy, an old man named Paulus. He said that when young he had met at Rome with an aged amanuensis of the blessed Cyprian, who told him that Cyprian never passed a day without reading some portion of Tertullian's works, and used frequently to say, *Give me my master*, meaning Tertullian. After remaining a presbyter of the church until he had attained the middle age of life, Tertullian was, by the envy and contumelious treatment of the Roman clergy, driven to embrace the opinions of Montanus, which he has mentioned in several of his works under the title of the New Prophecy....He is reported to have lived to a very advanced age, and to have composed many other works which are not extant." We add Bishop Kaye's notes on this extract, in an abridged shape: "The correctness of some parts of this account has been questioned. Doubts have been entertained whether Tertullian was a presbyter, although these have solely arisen from Roman Catholic objections to a married priesthood; for it is certain that he was married, there being among his works two treatises addressed to his wife....Another question has been raised respecting the place where Tertullian officiated as a presbyter—whether at Carthage or at Rome. That he at one time resided at Carthage may be inferred from Jerome's statement, and is rendered certain by several passages of his own writings. Allix supposes that the notion of his having been a presbyter of the Roman Church owed its rise to what Jerome said of the envy and abuse of the Roman clergy impelling him to espouse the party of Montanus. Optatus, and the author of the work *de Hæresibus*, which Sirmond edited under the title of Prædestinatus, expressly call him a Carthaginian presbyter. Semler, however, in a dissertation inserted in his edition of Tertullian's works, contends that he was a presbyter of the Roman Church. Eusebius tells us that he was accurately acquainted with the Roman laws, and on other accounts a distinguished person at Rome. Tertullian displays, moreover, a knowledge of the proceedings of the Roman Church with respect to Marcion and Valentinus, who were once members of it, which could scarcely have been obtained by one who had not himself been numbered amongst its presbyters Semler admits that, after Tertullian seceded from the church, he left and returned to Carthage. Jerome does not inform us whether Tertullian was born of Christian parents, or was converted to Christianity. There are passages in his writings which seem to imply that he had been a Gentile; yet he may perhaps mean to describe, not his own condition, but that of Gentiles in general, before their conversion. Allix and the majority of commentators understand them literally, as well as some other passages in which he speaks of his own infirmities and sinfulness. His writings show that he flourished at the period specified by Jerome—that is, during the reigns of Severus and Antoninus Caracalla, or between the years a.d. 193 and 216; but they supply no precise information respecting the date of his birth, or any of the principal occurrences of his life. Allix places his birth about 145 or 150; his conversion to Christianity about a.d. 185; his marriage about 186; his admission to the priesthood about 192; his adoption of the opinions of Montanus about 199; and his death about a.d. 220.

But these dates, it must be understood, rest entirely on conjecture."

(II.) Tertullian's work against Marcion, as it happens, is, *as to its date*, the best authenticated—perhaps the only well authenticated—particular connected with the author's life.
He himself mentions the fifteenth year of the reign of Severus as the time when he was writing the work: "Ad xv. jam Severi imperatoris." This agrees with Jerome's Chronicle, where occurs this note: "Anno 2223 Severi xv° Tertullianus...celebratur." This year is assigned to the year of our Lord 207; but notwithstanding the certainty of this date, it is far from clear that it describes more than the time of the publication of *the first book*. On the contrary, it is nearly certain that the other books, although connected manifestly enough in the author's argument and purpose (compare the initial and the final chapters of the several books), were yet issued at separate times. Noesselt shows that between the Book i. and Books ii.–iv. Tertullian issued his *De Præscript. Hæret.*, and previous to Book v. he published his tracts, *De Carne Christi* and *De Resurrectione Carnis*. After giving the incontestable date of the xv. of Severus for the first book, he says it is a mistake to suppose that the other books were published with it. He adds: "Although we cannot undertake to determine whether Tertullian issued his Books ii., iii., iv., against Marcion, together or separately, or in what year, we yet venture to affirm that Book v. appeared apart from the rest. For the tract *De Resurr. Carnis* appears from its second chapter to have been published after the tract *De Carne Christi*, in which latter work (chap. vii.) he quotes a passage from the fourth book against Marcion. But in his Book v. against Marcion (chap. x.), he refers to his work *De Resurr. Carnis*; which circumstance makes it evident that Tertullian published his Book v. at a different time from his Book iv. In his Book i. he announces his intention (chap. i.) of some time or other completing his tract *De Præscript. Hæret.*, but in his book *De Carne Christi* (chap. ii.), he mentions how he had completed

it,—a conclusive proof that his Book i. against Marcion preceded the other books."

(III.) Respecting Marcion himself, the most formidable heretic who had as yet opposed revealed truth, enough will turn up in this treatise, with the notes which we have added in explanation, to satisfy the reader. It will, however, be convenient to give here a few introductory particulars of him. Tertullian mentions Marcion as being, with Valentinus, in communion with the Church at Rome, "under the episcopate of the blessed Eleutherus." He goes on to charge them with "ever-restless curiosity, with which they infected even the brethren;" and informs us that they were more than once put out of communion—"Marcion, indeed, with the 200 sesterces which he brought into the church." He goes on to say, that "being at last condemned to the banishment of a perpetual separation, they sowed abroad the poisons of their doctrines. Afterwards, when Marcion, having professed penitence, agreed to the terms offered to him, that he should receive reconciliation on condition that he brought back to the church the rest also, whom he had trained up for perdition, he was prevented by death." He was a native of Sinope in Pontus, of which city, according to an account preserved by Epiphanius, which, however, is somewhat doubtful, his father was bishop, and of high character both for his orthodoxy and exemplary practice. He came to Rome soon after the death of Hyginus, probably about a.d. 141 or 142; and soon after his arrival he adopted the heresy of Cerdon.

(IV.) It is an interesting question as to what edition of the Holy Scriptures Tertullian used in his very copious quotations. It may at once be asserted that he did not cite from the Hebrew, although some writers have claimed for him, among his varied learning, a knowledge of the sacred language. Bp. Kaye observes, page 61, n. 1, that "he sometimes speaks as if he was acquainted with Hebrew," and refers to the *Anti-Marcion* iv. 39, the *Adv. Praxeam* v., and the *Adv. Judæos* ix. Be this as it may, it is manifest that Tertullian's Scripture passages never resemble the Hebrew, but in nearly every instance the Septuagint, whenever, as is most frequently the case, that version differs from the original. In the New Testament there is, as might be expected, a tolerably close conformity to the Greek. There is, however, it must be allowed, a sufficiently frequent variation from the letter of both the Greek Testaments to justify Semler's suspicion that Tertullian always quoted from the old Latin version, whatever that might have been, which was current in the African church in the second and third centuries. The most valuable part of Semler's *Dissertatio de varia et incerta indole Librorum Q. S. F. Tertulliani* is his investigation of this very point. In section iv. he endeavors to prove this proposition: "Hic scriptor non in manibus habuit Græcos libros sacros;" and he states his conclusion thus: "Certissimum est nec Tertullianum nec Cyprianum nec ullum scriptorem e Latinis illis ecclesiasticis provocare unquam ad Græcorum librorum auctoritatem si vel maxime obscura aut contraria lectio occurreret;" and again: "Ex his satis certum est, Latinos satis diu secutos fuisse auctoritatem suorum librorum adversus Græcos, nec concessisse nisi serius, cum Augustini et Hieronymi nova auctoritas juvare videretur." It is not ignorance of Greek which is imputed to Tertullian, for he is said to have well understood that language, and even to have composed in it. He probably followed the Latin, as writers now usually quote the authorized English, as being current and best known among their readers. Independent feeling, also, would have weight with such a temper as Tertullian's, to say nothing of the suspicion which largely prevailed in the African branch of the Latin church, that the Greek copies of the Scriptures were much corrupted by the heretics, who were chiefly, if not wholly, Greeks or Greek-speaking persons.

(V.) Whatever perverting effect Tertullian's secession to the sect of Montanus may have had on his judgment in his latest writings, it did not vitiate the work against Marcion. With a few trivial exceptions, this treatise may be read by the strictest Catholic without any feeling of annoyance. His lapse to Montanism is set down conjecturally as having taken place a.d. 199. Jerome, we have seen, attributed the event to his quarrel with the Roman clergy, but this is at least doubtful; nor must it be forgotten that Tertullian's mind seems to have been peculiarly suited by nature to adopt the mystical notions and ascetic principles of Montanus. It is satisfactory to find that, on the whole, "the authority of Tertullian," as the learned Dr. Burton says, "upon great points of doctrine is considered to be little, if at all, affected by his becoming a Montanist." (*Lectures on Eccl. Hist.* vol. ii. p. 234.) Besides the different works which are expressly mentioned in the notes of this volume, recourse has been had by the translator to Dupin's *Hist. Eccl. Writers* (trans.), vol. i. pp. 69–86; Tillemont's *Mèmoires Hist. Eccl.* iii. 85–103; Dr. Smith's *Greek and Roman Biography*, articles "Marcion" and "Tertullian;" Schaff's article, in Herzog's *Cyclopædia*, on "Tertullian;" Munter's *Primordia Eccl. Africanæ*, pp. 118–150; Robertson's *Church Hist.* vol. i. pp. 70–77; Dr. P. Schaff's *Hist. of Christian Church* (New York, 1859, pp. 511–519), and Archdeacon Evans' *Biography of the Early Church*, vol. i. (Lives of "Marcion," pp. 93–122, and "Tertullian," pp. 325–363). This last work, though of a popular cast, shows a good deal of research and learning, expressed in the pleasant style of the once popular author of *The Rectory of Vale Head*. The translator has mentioned these works, because they are all quite accessible to the general reader, and will give him adequate information concerning the subject treated in the present volume.

To this introduction of Dr. Holmes must be added that of Mr. Thelwall, the translator of the Third volume in the Edinburgh Series, as follows:

To arrange chronologically the works (especially if numerous) of an author whose own date is known with tolerable precision, is not always or necessarily easy: witness the controversies as to the succession of St. Paul's epistles. To do this in the case of an author whose own date is itself a matter of controversy may therefore be reasonably expected to be still less so; and such is the predicament of him who attempts to perform this task for Tertullian. I propose to give a specimen or two of the difficulties with which the task is beset; and then to lay before the reader briefly a summary of the results at which eminent scholars, who have devoted much time and thought to the subject, have arrived. Such a course, I think, will at once afford him means of judging of the absolute impossibility of arriving at definite certainty in the matter; and induce him to excuse me if I prefer furnishing him with materials from which to deduce his own conclusions, rather than venturing on an *ex cathedra* decision on so doubtful a subject.

I. The book, as Dr. Holmes has reminded us, of the date of which we seem to have the surest evidence, is *Adv. Marc.* i. This book was in course of writing, as its author himself (c. 15) tells us, "in the fifteenth year of the empire of Severus." Now this date would be clear if there were no doubt as to which year of our era corresponds to Tertullian's fifteenth of Severus. Pamelius, however, says Dr. Holmes, makes it a.d. 208; Clinton, (whose authority is more recent and better,) 207.

2. Another book which promises to give some clue to its date is the *de Pallio*. The writer uses these phrases: "præsentis imperii *triplex virtus*;" "Deo *tot Augustis in unum* favente;" which show that there were at the time three persons unitedly bearing the title *Augusti*—not *Cæsares* only, but the still higher *Augusti*;—while the remainder of that context, as well as the opening of c. 1, indicates a time of peace of some considerable duration; a time of plenty; and a time during and previous to which great changes had taken place in the general aspect of the Roman Empire, and some particular traitor had been discovered and frustrated. Such a combination of circumstances might seem to fix the date with some degree of assurance. But unhappily, as Kaye reminds us, commentators cannot agree as to who the three Augusti are. Some say

Severus, Caracalla, and *Albinus*; some say Severus, Caracalla, and *Geta*. Hence we have a difference of some twelve years or thereabouts in the computations. For Albinus was defeated by Severus in person, and fell by his own hand, in a.d. 197; and Geta, Severus' second son, brother of Caracalla, was not associated by his father with himself and his other son as *Augustus* until a.d. 208, though he had received the title of *Cæsar* ten years before, in the same year in which *Caracalla* had received that of Augustus. For my own part, I may perhaps be allowed to say that I should incline to agree, like Salmasius, with those who assign the later date. The limits of the present Introduction forbid my entering at large into my reasons for so doing. I am, however, supported in it by the authority of Neander. In one point, though, I should hesitate to agree with Oehler, who appears to follow Salmasius and others herein,—namely, in understanding the expression "et cacto et rubo subdolæ familiaritatis convulso" of *Albinus*. It seems to me the words might with more propriety be applied to *Plautianus*; and that in the word "familiaritatis" we may see (after Tertullian's fashion) a play upon the meaning, with a reference not only to the long-standing but mischievous *intimacy* which existed between Severus and his countryman (perhaps fellow-townsman) Plautianus, who for his harshness and cruelty is fitly compared to the prickly *cactus*. He alludes likewise to the alliance which this ambitious prætorian præfect had contrived to contract with the *family* of the emperor, by the marriage of his daughter Plautilla to Caracalla,—an event which, as it turned out, led to his own death. Thus in the "*rubo*" there may be a reference to the ambitious and conceited "bramble" of Jotham's parable, and perhaps, too, to the "thistle" of Jehoash's. If this be so, the date would be at least approximately fixed, as Plautianus did not marry his daughter to Caracalla till a.d. 203, and was himself put to death in the following year, 204, while Geta, as we have seen, was made Augustus in 208.

3. The date of the *Apology*, however, is perhaps at once the most contested, and the most strikingly illustrative of the

difficulties to which allusion has been made. It is not surprising that its date *should* have been more disputed than that of other pieces, inasmuch as it is the best known, and (for some reasons) the most interesting and famous, of all our author's productions. In fact, the dates assigned to it by different authorities vary from Mosheim's 198 to that suggested by the very learned Allix, who assigns it to 217.

4. Once more. In the tract *de Monogamia* (c. 3) the author says that since the date of St. Paul's first Epistle to the Corinthians "about 160 years had elapsed." Here, again, did we only know with certainty the precise date of that epistle, we could ascertain "about" the date of the tract. But (a) the date of the epistle is itself variously given, Burton giving it as early as a.d. 52, Michaelis and Mill as late as 57; and (b) Tertullian only says, "Armis *circiter* clx. exinde productis;" while the way in which, in the *ad Natt.*, within the short space of three chapters, he states first that 250, and then (in c. 9) that 300, years had not elapsed since the rise of the Christian name, leads us to think that here again he only desires to speak in round numbers, meaning perhaps *more* than 150, but *less* than 170.

These specimens must suffice, though it might be easy to add to them. There is, however, another classification of our author's writings which has been attempted. Finding the haplessness of strict chronological accuracy, commentators have seized on the idea that peradventure there might be found at all events some internal marks by which to determine which of them were written before, which after, the writer's secession to Montanism. It may be confessed that this attempt has been somewhat more successful than the other. Yet even here there are two formidable obstacles standing in our way. The first and greatest is, that the natural temper of Tertullian was from the first so akin to the spirit of Montanism, that, unless there occur distinct allusions to the "New Prophecy," or expressions specially connected with Montanistic phraseology, the *general tone* of any treatise is not a very safe guide. The second is, that the subject-matter of some of the treatises is not such as to afford much scope for the introduction of the peculiarities of a sect which professed to differ in discipline only, not doctrine, from the church at large.

Still the result of this classification seems to show one important feature of agreement between commentators, however they may differ upon details; and that is, that considerably the larger part of our author's rather voluminous productions must have been subsequent to his lamented secession. I think the best way to give the reader means for forming his own judgment will be, as I have said, to lay before him in parallel columns a tabular view of the disposition of the books by Dr. Neander and Bishop Kaye. These two modern writers, having given particular care to the subject, bringing to bear upon it all the advantages derived from wide reading, eminent abilities, and a diligent study of the works of preceding writers on the same questions, have a special right to be heard upon the matter in hand; and I think, if I may be allowed to say so, that, for calm judgment, and minute acquaintance with his author, I shall not be accused of undue partiality if I express my opinion that, as far as my own observation goes, the palm must be awarded to the Bishop. In this view I am supported by the fact that the accomplished Professor Ramsay, follows Dr. Kaye's arrangement. I premise that Dr. Neander adopts a threefold division, into:

1. Writings which were occasioned by the relation of the Christians to the heathen, and refer to their vindication of Christianity against the heathen; attacks on heathenism; the sufferings and conduct of Christians under persecution; and the intercourse of Christians with heathens:

2. Writings which relate to Christian and church life, and to ecclesiastical discipline:

3. The dogmatic and dogmatico-controversial treatises.

And under each head he subdivides into:

a. Pre-Montanist writings; b. Post-Montanist writings: thus leaving no room for what Kaye calls "works respecting which nothing certain can be pronounced." For the sake of clearness, this order has not been followed in the table. On the other side, it will be seen that Dr. Kaye, while not assuming to speak with more than a reasonable probability, is careful so to arrange the treatises under each head as to show the order, so far as it is discoverable, in which the books under that head were published; i.e., if one book is quoted in another book, the book so quoted, if distinctly referred to as already before the world, is plainly anterior to that in which it is quoted. Thus, then, have:

Neander.
I. *Pre-Montanist.*
1. De Poenitentia.
2. De Oratione.
3. De Baptismo.
4. Ad Uxorem i.
5. Ad Uxorem ii.
6. Ad Martyres.
7. De Patientia.
8. De Spectaculis.
9. De Idololatria.
10. 11. Ad Nationes i. ii.
12. Apologeticus.
13. De Testimonio Animæ.
14. De Præscr. Hæreticorum.
15. De Cult. Fem. i.
16. De Cult. Fem. ii.
II. *Montanist.*
17–21. Adv. Marc. i. ii. iii. iv. v.
22. De Anima.
23. De Carne Christi.
24. De Res. Carn.
25. De Cor. Mil.
26. De Virg. Vel.
27. De Ex. Cast.

28. De Monog.
29. De Jejuniis.
30. De Pudicitia.
31. De Pallio.
32. Scorpiace.
33. Ad Scapulam.
34. Adv. Valentinianos.
35. Adv. Hermogenem.
36. Adv. Praxeam.
37. Adv. Judæos.
38. De Fuga in Persecutione.

Kaye.

I. *Pre-Montanist* (probably).

1. De Poenitentia.
2. De Oratione.
3. De Baptismo.
4. Ad Uxorem i.
5. Ad Uxorem ii.
6. Ad Martyres.
7. De Patientia.
8. Adv. Judæos.
9. De Præscr. Hæreticorum.

II. *Montanist* (certainly).

10. Adv. Marc. i.
11. Adv. Marc. ii.
12. De Anima.
13. Adv. Marc. iii.
14. Adv. Marc. iv.
15. De Carne Christi.
16. De Resurrectione Carnis.
17. Adv. Marc. v.
18. Adv. Praxeam.
19. Scorpiace.
20. De Corona Militis.
21. De Virginibus Velandis.
22. De Exhortatione Castitatis.

23. De Fuga in Persecutione.
24. De Monogamia.
25. De Jejuniis.
26. De Pudicitia.
III. *Montanist* (probably).
27. Adv. Valentinianos.
28. Ad Scapulam.
29. De Spectaculis.
30. De Idololatria.
31. De Cultu Feminarum i.
32. De Cultu Feminarum ii.
IV. *Works respecting which nothing certain can be pronounced.*
33. The Apology.
34. Ad Nationes i.
35. Ad Nationes ii.
36. De Testimonio Animæ.
37. De Pallio.
38. Adv. Hermogenem.

A comparison of these two lists will show that the difference between the two great authorities is, as Kaye remarks, "not great; and with respect to some of the tracts on which we differ, the learned author expresses himself with great diffidence." The main difference, in fact, is that which affects two tracts upon kindred subjects, the *de Spectaculis*, and *Idololatria*, the *de Cultu Feminarum* (a subject akin to the other two), and the *adv. Judæos*. With reference to all these, except the last, to which I believe the Archdeacon does not once refer, the Bishop's opinion appears to have the support of Archdeacon Evans, whose learned and interesting essay, referred to in the note, appears in a volume published in 1837. Dr. Kaye's Lectures, on which his book is founded, were delivered in 1825. Of the date of his first edition I am not aware. Dr. Neander's *Antignostikus* also first appeared in 1825. The preface to his second edition bears date July 1, 1849. As to the *adv. Judæos*, I confess I agree with Neander in thinking that, at all events from the beginning of c. 9, it is spurious. If it be urged that Jerome expressly quotes it as Tertullian's, I reply, Jerome so quotes it, I believe, when he is expounding *Daniel*. Now all that the *adv. Jud.* has to say about *Daniel* ends with the end of c. 8. It is therefore quite compatible with the fact thus stated to recognize the earlier half of the book as genuine, and to reject the rest, beginning, as it happens, just after the eighth chapter, as spurious. Perhaps Dr. Neander's Jewish birth and training peculiarly fit him to be heard on this question. Nor do I think Professor Ramsay (in the article above alluded to) has quite seen the force of Kaye's own remarks on Neander.What he does say is equally creditable to his candor and his accuracy; namely: "The instances alleged by Dr. Neander, in proof of this position, are undoubtedly very remarkable; but if the concluding chapters of the tract are spurious, no ground seems to be left for asserting that the genuine portion was posterior to the third Book against Marcion,—and none, consequently, for asserting that it was written by a Montanist." With which remark I must draw these observations on the genuine extant works of Tertullian to a close.

The next point to which a brief reference must be made is the *lost works* of Tertullian, lists of these are given both by Oehler and by Kaye, viz.:

1. A Book on Aaron's Robes: mentioned by Jerome, Epist. 128, *ad Fabiolam de Veste Sacerdotali* (tom. ii. p. 586, Opp. ed. Bened.).

2. A Book on the Superstition of the Age.

3. A Book on the Submission of the Soul.

4. A Book on the Flesh and the Soul.

Nos. 2, 3, and 4 are known only by their titles, which are found in the Index to Tertullian's works given in the *Codex Agobardi*; but the tracts themselves are not extant in the ms., which appears to have once contained—

5. A Book on Paradise, named in the Index, and referred to in *de Anima* 55, *adv. Marc*. iii. 12; and

6. A Book on the Hope of the Faithful: also named in the Index, and referred to *adv. Marc.* iii. 24; and by Jerome in his account of Papias, and on Ezek. xxxvi.; and by Gennadius of Marseilles.

7. Six Books on Ecstasy, with a seventh in reply to Apollonius: see Jerome. See, too, J. A. Fabricius on the words of the unknown author whom the Jesuit Sirmond edited under the name *Prædestinatus*; who gathers thence that "Soter, pope of the City, and Apollonius, bishop of the Ephesians, wrote a book against the Montanists; *in reply to whom* Tertullian, a Carthaginian presbyter, wrote." J. Pamelius thinks these seven books were originally published *in Greek.*

8. A Book in reply to the Apellesites (i.e. the followers of Apelles): referred to in *de Carne Christi*, c. 8.

9. A Book on the Origin of the Soul, in reply to Hermogenes: referred to in *de Anima*, cc. 1, 3, 22, 24.

10. A Book on Fate: referred to by Fulgentius Planciades, p. 562, Merc.; also referred to as either written, or intended to be written, by Tertullian himself, *de Anima*, c. 20. Jerome states that there was extant, or had been extant, a book on Fate under the name of Minucius Felix, written indeed by a perspicuous author, but not in the style of Minucius Felix. This, Pamelius judged, should perhaps be rather ascribed to Tertullian.

11. A Book on the Trinity. Jerome says: "Novatian wrote....a large volume on the Trinity, *as if making an epitome of a work of Tertullian's, which most men not knowing regard it as Cyprian's.*" Novatian's book stood in Tertullian's name in the mss. of J. Gangneius, who was the first to edit it; in a Malmesbury ms. which Sig. Gelenius used; and in others.

12. A Book addressed to a Philosophic Friend on the Straits of Matrimony. Both Kaye and Oehler are in doubt whether Jerome's words, by which some have been led to conclude that Tertullian wrote some book or books on this and kindred subjects, really imply as much, or whether they may not refer merely to those tracts and passages in his extant writings which touch upon such matters. Kaye hesitates to

think that the "Book to a Philosophic Friend" is the same as the *de Exhortatione Castitatis*, because Jerome says Tertullian wrote on the subject of celibacy "*in his youth*;" but as Cave takes what Jerome elsewhere says of Tertullian's leaving the Church "*about the middle of his age*" to mean his *spiritual age*, the same sense might attach to his words here too, and thus obviate the Bishop's difficulty.

There are some other works which have been attributed to Tertullian—on Circumcision; on Animals Clean and Unclean; on the truth that God is a Judge—which Oehler likewise rejects, believing that the expressions of Jerome refer only to passages in the *Anti-Marcion* and other extant works. To Novatian Jerome does ascribe a distinct work on Circumcision, and this may (comp. 11, just above) have given rise to the view that Tertullian had written one also.

There were, moreover, three treatises at least written by Tertullian *in Greek*. They are:

1. A Book on Public Shows. See *de Cor*. c. 6.
2. A Book on Baptism. See *de Bapt*. c. 15.
3. A Book on the Veiling of Virgins. See de *V. V.* c. 1.

Oehler adds that J. Pamelius, in his epistle dedicatory to Philip II. of Spain, makes mention of a *Greek copy* of Tertullian in the library of that king. This report, however, since nothing has ever been seen or heard of the said copy from that time, Oehler judges to be erroneous.

It remains briefly to notice the confessedly spurious works which the editions of Tertullian generally have appended to them. With these Kaye does not deal. The fragment, *adv. omnes Hæreses*, Oehler attributes to Victorinus Petavionensis, i.e., Victorinus bishop of Pettaw, on the Drave, in Austrian Styria. It was once thought he ought to be called *Pictaviensis*, i.e. of *Poictiers*; but John Launoy has shown this to be an error. Victorinus is said by Jerome to have "understood Greek better than Latin; hence his works are excellent for the sense, but mean as to the style." Cave believes him to have been a Greek by birth. Cassiodorus states him to have been once a professor of rhetoric. Jerome's statement agrees with the style of the tract in question; and Jerome distinctly says Victorinus did write *adversus omnes Hæreses*. Allix leaves the question of its authorship quite uncertain. If Victorinus be the author, the book falls clearly within the Ante-Nicene period; for Victorinus fell a martyr in the Diocletian persecution, probably about a.d. 303.

The next fragment—"Of the Execrable Gods of the Heathens"—is of quite uncertain authorship. Oehler would attribute it "to some declaimer not quite ignorant of Tertullian's writings," but certainly not to Tertullian himself.

Lastly we come to the metrical fragments. Concerning these, it is perhaps impossible to assign them to their rightful owners. Oehler has not troubled himself much about them; but he seems to regard the *Jonah* as worthy of more regard than the rest, for he seems to have intended giving more labor to its editing at some future time. Whether he has ever done so, or given us his German version of Tertullian's own works, which, "si Deus adjuverit," he distinctly promises in his preface, I do not know. Perhaps the best thing to be done under the circumstances is to give the judgment of the learned Peter Allix. It may be premised that by the celebrated George Fabricius—who published his great work, *Poetarum Veterum Ecclesiasticorum Opera Christiana*, etc., in 1564—the *Five Books in Reply to Marcion*, and the *Judgment of the Lord*, are ascribed to Tertullian, the *Genesis* and *Sodom* to Cyprian. Pamelius likewise seems to have ascribed the *Five Books*, the *Jonah*, and the *Sodom* to Tertullian; and according to Lardner, Bishop Bull likewise attributed the *Five Books* to him. They have been generally ascribed to the Victorinus above mentioned. Tillemont, among others, thinks they may well enough be his. Rigaltius is content to demonstrate that they are not Tertullian's, but leaves the real authorship without attempting to decide it. Of the others the same eminent critic says, "They seem to have been written at Carthage, at an age not far removed from Tertullian's." Allix, after observing that

Pamelius is inconsistent with himself in attributing the *Genesis* and *Sodom* at one time to Tertullian, at another to Cyprian, rejects both views equally, and assigns the Genesis with some confidence to Salvian, a presbyter of Marseilles, whose "floruit" Cave gives *cir.* 440, a contemporary of Gennadius, and a copious author. To this it is, Allix thinks, that Gennadius alludes in his *Catalogue of Illustrious Men*, c. 77.

The *Judgment of the Lord* Allix ascribes to one Verecundus, an African bishop, whose date he finds it difficult to decide exactly. He refers to two of the name: one Bishop of Tunis, whom Victor of Tunis in his chronicle mentions as having died in exile at Chalcedon a.d. 552; the other Bishop of Noba, who visited Carthage with many others a.d. 482, at the summons of King Huneric, to answer there for their faith;—and would ascribe the poem to the former, thinking that he finds an allusion to it in the article upon that Verecundus in the *de Viris Illustribus* of Isidore of Seville. Oehler agrees with him. The *Five Books* Allix seems to hint may be attributed to some imitator of the Victorinus of Pettaw named above.
Oehler attributes them rather to one Victorinus, or Victor, of Marseilles, a rhetorician, who died a.d. 450. He appears in G. Fabricius as Claudius Marius Victorinus, writer of a *Commentary on Genesis*, and an epistle *ad Salomonem Abbata*, both in verse, and of some considerable length.

The Chaplet, or De Corona.

Chapter I.

Very lately it happened thus: while the bounty of our most excellent emperors was dispensed in the camp, the soldiers, laurel-crowned, were approaching. One of them, more a soldier of God, more steadfast than the rest of his brethren, who had imagined that they could serve two masters, his head alone uncovered, the useless crown in his hand—already even by that peculiarity known to everyone as a Christian—was nobly conspicuous. Accordingly, all began to mark him out, jeering him at a distance, gnashing on him near at hand.
The murmur is wafted to the tribune, when the person had just left the ranks. The tribune at once puts the question to him, Why are you so different in your attire? He declared that he had no liberty to wear the crown with the rest. Being urgently asked for his reasons, he answered, I am a Christian. O soldier! boasting thyself in God. Then the case was considered and voted on; the matter was remitted to a higher tribunal; the offender was conducted to the prefects. At once he put away the heavy cloak, his disburdening commenced; he loosed from his foot the military shoe, beginning to stand upon holy ground; he gave up the sword, which was not necessary either for the protection of our Lord; from his hand likewise dropped the laurel crown; and now, purple-clad with the hope of his own blood, shod with the preparation of the gospel, girt with the sharper word of God, completely equipped in the apostles' armor, and crowned more worthily with the white crown of martyrdom, he awaits in prison the largess of Christ. Thereafter adverse judgments began to be passed upon his conduct—whether on the part of Christians I do not know, for those of the heathen are not different—as if he were headstrong and rash, and too eager to die, because, in being taken to task about a mere matter of dress, he brought trouble on the bearers of the Name,—he, forsooth, alone brave among so many soldier-

brethren, he alone a Christian. It is plain that as they have rejected the prophecies of the Holy Spirit, they are also purposing the refusal of martyrdom. So they murmur that a peace so good and long is endangered for them. Nor do I doubt that some are already turning their back on the Scriptures, are making ready their luggage, are equipped for flight from city to city; for that is all of the gospel they care to remember. I know, too, their pastors are lions in peace, deer in the fight. As to the questions asked for extorting confessions from us, we shall teach elsewhere. Now, as they put forth also the objection—But where are we forbidden to be crowned?—I shall take this point up, as more suitable to be treated of here, being the essence, in fact, of the present contention. So that, on the one hand, the inquirers who are ignorant, but anxious, may be instructed; and on the other, those may be refuted who try to vindicate the sin, especially the laurel-crowned Christians themselves, to whom it is merely a question of debate, as if it might be regarded as either no trespass at all, or at least a doubtful one, because it may be made the subject of investigation. That it is neither sinless nor doubtful, I shall now, however, show.

Chapter II.

I affirm that not one of the Faithful has ever a crown upon his head, except at a time of trial. That is the case with all, from catechumens to confessors and martyrs, or (as the case may be) deniers. Consider, then, whence the custom about which we are now chiefly inquiring got its authority. But when the question is raised why it is observed, it is meanwhile evident that it is observed. Therefore that can neither be regarded as no offence, or an uncertain one, which is perpetrated against a practice which is capable of defense, on the ground even of its repute, and is sufficiently ratified by the support of general acceptance. It is undoubted, so that we ought to inquire into the reason of the thing; but without prejudice to the practice, not for the purpose of overthrowing it, but rather of building it up, that you may all the more carefully observe it, when you are also satisfied as to its reason. But what sort of procedure is it, for one to be bringing into debate a practice, when he has fallen from it, and to be seeking the explanation of his having ever had it, when he has left it off? Since, although he may wish to seem on this account desirous to investigate it, that he may show that he has not done wrong in giving it up, it is evident that he nevertheless transgressed previously in its presumptuous observance. If he has done no wrong to-day in accepting the crown he offended before in refusing it. This treatise, therefore, will not be for those who not in a proper condition for inquiry, but for those who, with the real desire of getting instruction, bring forward, not a question for debate, but a request for advice. For it is from this desire that a true inquiry always proceeds; and I praise the faith which has believed in the duty of complying with the rule, before it has learned the reason of it. An easy thing it is at once to demand where it is written that we should not be crowned. But is it written that we should be crowned? Indeed, in urgently demanding the warrant of Scripture in a different side from their own, men prejudge that the support of Scripture ought no less to appear on their part. For if it shall be said that it is lawful to be crowned on this ground, that Scripture does not forbid it, it will as validly be retorted that just on this ground is the crown unlawful, because the Scripture does not enjoin it. What shall discipline do? Shall it accept both things, as if neither were forbidden? Or shall it refuse both, as if neither were enjoined? But "the thing which is not forbidden is freely permitted." I should rather say that what has not been freely allowed is forbidden.

Chapter III.

And how long shall we draw the saw to and fro through this line, when we have an ancient practice, which by anticipation has made for us the state, i.e., of the question? If no passage of Scripture has prescribed it, assuredly custom, which without doubt flowed from tradition, has confirmed it. For how can anything come into use, if it has not first been handed down? Even in pleading tradition, written authority, you say, must be demanded. Let us inquire, therefore, whether tradition, unless it be written, should not be admitted.

Certainly we shall say that it ought not to be admitted, if no cases of other practices which, without any written instrument, we maintain on the ground of tradition alone, and the countenance thereafter of custom, affords us any precedent. To deal with this matter briefly, I shall begin with baptism. When we are going to enter the water, but a little before, in the presence of the congregation and under the hand of the president, we solemnly profess that we disown the devil, and his pomp, and his angels. Hereupon we are thrice immersed, making a somewhat ampler pledge than the Lord has appointed in the Gospel. Then when we are taken up (as new-born children), we taste first of all a mixture of milk and honey, and from that day we refrain from the daily bath for a whole week. We take also, in congregations before daybreak, and from the hand of none but the presidents, the sacrament of the Eucharist, which the Lord both commanded to be eaten at meal-times, and enjoined to be taken by all alike. As often as the anniversary comes around, we make offerings for the dead as birthday honors. We count fasting or kneeling in worship on the Lord's day to be unlawful. We rejoice in the same privilege also from Easter to Whitsunday. We feel pained should any wine or bread, even though our own, be cast upon the ground. At every forward step and movement, at every going in and out, when we put on our clothes and shoes, when we bathe, when we sit at table, when we light the lamps, on couch, on seat, in all the ordinary actions of daily life, we trace upon the forehead the sign.

Chapter IV.

If, for these and other such rules, you insist upon having positive Scripture injunction, you will find none. Tradition will be held forth to you as the originator of them, custom as their strengthener, and faith as their observer. That reason will support tradition, and custom, and faith, you will either yourself perceive, or learn from someone who has. Meanwhile you will believe that there is some reason to which submission is due. I add still one case more, as it will be proper to show you how it was among the ancients also. Among the Jews, so usual is it for their women to have the head veiled, that they may thereby be recognized. I ask in this instance for the law. I put the apostle aside. If Rebecca at once drew down her veil, when in the distance she saw her betrothed, this modesty of a mere private individual could not have made a law, or it will have made it only for those who have the reason which she had. Let virgins alone be veiled, and this when they are coming to be married, and not till they have recognized their destined husband. If Susanna also, who was subjected to unveiling on her trial, furnishes an argument for the veiling of women, I can say here also, the veil was a voluntary thing. She had come accused, ashamed of the disgrace she had brought on herself, properly concealing her beauty, even because now she feared to please. But I should not suppose that, when it was her aim to please, she took walks with a veil on in her husband's avenue. Grant, now, that she was always veiled. In this particular case, too, or, in fact, in that of any other, I demand the dress-law. If I nowhere find a law, it follows that tradition has given the fashion in question to custom, to find subsequently (its authorization in) the apostle's sanction, from the true interpretation of reason. This instances, therefore, will make it sufficiently plain that you can vindicate the keeping of even unwritten tradition established by custom; the proper witness for tradition when demonstrated by long-continued observance. But even in civil matters custom is accepted as law, when positive legal enactment is wanting; and it is the same thing whether it depends on writing or on reason, since reason is, in fact, the basis of law. But, (you say), if reason is the ground of law, all will now henceforth have to be counted law, whoever brings it forward, which shall have reason as its ground. Or do you think that every believer is entitled to originate and establish a law, if only it be such as is agreeable to God, as is helpful to discipline, as promotes salvation, when the Lord says, "But why do you not even of your own selves judge what is right?" And not merely in regard to a judicial sentence, but in regard to every decision in matters we are called on to consider, the apostle also says, "If of anything you are ignorant, God shall reveal it unto you;" he himself, too, being accustomed to afford counsel though he had not the command of the Lord, and to dictate of himself as possessing the Spirit of God who guides into all truth. Therefore his advice has, by the warrant of divine reason, become equivalent to nothing less than a divine command. Earnestly now inquire of this teacher, keeping intact your regard for tradition, from whomsoever it originally sprang; nor have regard to the author, but to the authority, and especially that of custom itself, which on this very account we should revere, that we may not want an interpreter; so that if reason too is God's gift, you may then learn, not whether custom has to be followed by you, but why.

Chapter V.

The argument for Christian practices becomes all the stronger, when also nature, which is the first rule of all, supports them. Well, she is the first who lays it down that a crown does not become the head. But I think ours is the God of nature, who fashioned man; and, that he might desire, (appreciate, become partaker of) the pleasures afforded by His creatures, endowed him with certain senses, (acting) through members, which, so to speak, are their peculiar instruments. The sense of hearing he has planted in the ears; that of sight, lighted up in the eyes; that of taste, shut up in the mouth; that of smell, wafted into the nose; that of touch, fixed in the tips of the fingers. By means of these organs of the outer man doing duty to the inner man, the enjoyments of the divine gifts are conveyed by the senses to the soul. What, then, in flowers affords you enjoyment? For it is the flowers of the field which are the peculiar, at least the chief, material of crowns. Either smell, you say, or color, or both together. What will be the senses of color and smell? Those of seeing and smelling, I suppose. What members have had these senses allotted to them? The eyes and the nose, if I am not mistaken. With sight and smell, then, make use of flowers, for these are the senses by which they are meant to be enjoyed; use them by means of the eyes and nose, which are the members to which these senses belong. You have got the thing from God, the mode of it from the world; but an extraordinary mode does not prevent the use of the thing in the common way. Let flowers, then, both when fastened into each other and tied together in thread and rush, be what they are when free, when loose—things to be looked at and smelt. You count it a crown, let us say, when you have a bunch of them bound together in a series, that you may carry many at one time that you may enjoy them all at once. Well, lay them in your bosom if they are so singularly pure, and strew them on your couch if they are so exquisitely soft, and consign them to your cup if they are so perfectly harmless. Have the pleasure of them in as many ways as they appeal to your senses. But what taste for a flower, what sense for anything belonging to a crown but its band, have you in the head, which is able neither to distinguish color, nor to inhale sweet perfumes, nor to appreciate softness? It is as much against nature to long after a flower with the head, as it is to crave food with the ear, or sound with the nostril. But everything which is against nature deserves to be branded as monstrous among all men; but with us it is to be condemned also as sacrilege against God, the Lord and Creator of nature.

Chapter VI.

Demanding then a law of God, you have that common one prevailing all over the world, engraven on the natural tables to which the apostle too is wont to appeal, as when in respect of the woman's veil he says, "Does not even Nature teach you?"—as when to the Romans, affirming that the heathen do by nature those things which the law requires, he suggests both natural law and a law-revealing nature. Yes, and also in the first chapter of the epistle he authenticates nature, when he asserts that males and females changed among themselves the natural use of the creature into that which is unnatural, by way of penal retribution for their error. We first of all indeed know God Himself by the teaching of Nature, calling Him God of gods, taking for granted that He is good, and invoking Him as Judge. Is it a question with you whether for the enjoyment of His creatures, Nature should be our guide, that we may not be carried away in the direction in which the rival of God has corrupted, along with man himself, the entire creation which had been made over to our race for certain uses, whence the apostle says that it too unwillingly became subject to vanity, completely bereft of its original character, first by vain, then by base, unrighteous, and ungodly uses? It is thus, accordingly, in the pleasures of the shows, that the creature is dishonored by those who by nature indeed perceive that all the materials of which shows are got up belong to God, but lack the knowledge to perceive as well that they have all been changed by the devil. But with this topic we have, for the sake of our own play-lovers, sufficiently dealt, and that, too, in a work in Greek.

Chapter VII.

Let these dealers in crowns then recognize in the meantime the authority of Nature, on the ground of a common sense as human beings, and the certifications of their peculiar religion, as, according to the last chapter, worshippers of the God of nature; and, as it were, thus over and above what is required, let them consider those other reasons too which forbid us wearing crowns, especially on the head, and indeed crowns of every sort. For we are obliged to turn from the rule of Nature, which we share with mankind in general, that we may maintain the whole peculiarity of our Christian discipline, in relation also to other kinds of crowns which seem to have been provided for different uses, as being composed of different substances, lest, because they do not consist of flowers, the use of which nature has indicated (as it does in the case of this military laurel one itself), they may be thought not to come under the prohibition of our sect, since they have escaped any objections of nature. I see, then, that we must go into the matter both with more research, and more fully, from its beginnings on through its successive stages of growth to its more erratic developments. For this we need to turn to heathen literature, for things belonging to the heathen must be proved from their own documents. The little of this I have acquired, will, I believe, be enough. If there really was a Pandora, whom Hesiod mentions as the first of women, hers was the first head the graces crowned, for she received gifts from all *the gods* whence she got *her name* Pandora. But Moses, a prophet, not a poet-shepherd, shows us the first woman Eve having her loins more naturally girt about with leaves than her temples with flowers. Pandora, then, is a myth. And so we have to blush for the origin of the crown, even on the ground of the falsehood connected with it; and, as will soon appear, on the ground no less of its realities. For it is an undoubted fact that certain persons either originated the thing, or shed luster on it. Pherecydes relates that Saturn was the first who wore a crown; Diodorus, that Jupiter, after conquering the Titans, was honored with this gift by the rest of the gods. To Priapus also the same author assigns fillets; and to Ariadne a garland of gold and of Indian gems, the gift of Vulcan, afterwards of Bacchus, and subsequently turned into a constellation. Callimachus has put a vine crown upon Juno. So too at Argos, her statue, vine-wreathed, with a lion's skin placed beneath her feet, exhibits the stepmother exulting over the spoils of her two step-sons. Hercules displays upon his head sometimes poplar, sometimes wild olive, sometimes parsley. You have the tragedy of Cerberus; you have Pindar; and besides Callimachus, who mentions that Apollo, too when he had killed the Delphic serpent, as a suppliant, put on a laurel garland; for among the ancients suppliants were wont to be crowned. Harpocration argues that Bacchus the same as Osiris among the Egyptians, was designedly crowned with ivy, because it is the nature of ivy to protect the brain against drowsiness. But that in another way also Bacchus was the originator of the laurel crown (the crown) in which he celebrated his triumph over the Indians, even the rabble acknowledge, when they call the days dedicated to him the "great crown." If you open, again, the writings of the Egyptian Leo, you learn that Isis was the first who discovered and wore ears of corn upon her head—a thing more suited to the belly. Those who want additional information will find an ample exposition of the subject in Claudius Saturninus, a writer of distinguished talent who treats this question also, for he has a book on crowns, so explaining their beginnings as well as causes, and kinds, and rites, that you find all that is charming in the flower, all that is beautiful in the leafy branch, and every sod or vine-shoot has been dedicated to some head or other; making it abundantly clear how foreign to us we should judge the custom of the crowned head, introduced as it was by, and thereafter constantly managed for the honor of, those whom the world has believed to be gods. If the devil, a liar from the beginning, is even in this matter working for his false system of godhead (idolatry), he had himself also without doubt provided for his god-lie being carried out. What sort of thing, then, must that be counted among the people of the true God, which was brought in by the nations in honor of the devil's candidates, and was set apart from the beginning to no other than these; and which even then received its consecration to idolatry by idols and in idols yet alive? Not as if an idol were anything, but since the things which others offer up to idols belong to demons. But if the things which *others* offer to them belong to demons how much more what idols offered to themselves, when they were in life! The demons themselves, doubtless, had made provision for themselves by means of those whom they had possessed, while in a state of desire and craving, before provision had been actually made.

Chapter VIII.

Hold fast in the meantime this persuasion, while I examine a question which comes in our way. For I already hear it is said, that many other things as well as crowns have been invented by those whom the world believes to be gods, and that they are notwithstanding to be met with both in our present usages and in those of early saints, and in the service of God, and in Christ Himself, who did His work as man by no other than these ordinary instrumentalities of human life. Well, let it be so; nor shall I inquire any further back into the origin of this things. Let Mercury have been the first who taught the knowledge of letters; I will own that they are requisite both for the business and commerce of life, and for performing our devotion to God. Nay, if he also first strung the chord to give forth melody, I will not deny, when listening to David, that this invention has been in use with the saints, and has ministered to God. Let Æsculapius have been the first who sought and discovered cures: Esaias mentions that he ordered Hezekiah medicine when he was sick. Paul, too, knows that a little wine does the stomach good. Let Minerva have been the first who built a ship: I shall see Jonah and the apostles sailing. Nay, there is more than this: for even Christ, we shall find, has ordinary raiment; Paul, too, has his cloak. If at once, of every article of furniture and each household vessel, you name some god of the world as the originator, well, I must recognize Christ, both as He reclines on a couch, and when He presents a basin for the feet of His disciples, and when He pours water into it from a ewer, and when He is girt about with a linen towel—a garment especially sacred to Osiris. It is thus in general I reply upon the point, admitting indeed that we use along with others these articles, but challenging that this be judged in the light of the distinction between things agreeable and things opposed to reason, because the promiscuous employment of them is deceptive, concealing the corruption of the creature, by which it has been made subject to vanity. For we affirm that those things only are proper to be used, whether by ourselves or by those who lived before us, and alone befit the service of God and Christ Himself, which to meet the necessities of human life supply what is simply; useful and affords real assistance and honorable comfort, so that they may be well believed to have come from God's own inspiration, who first of all no doubt provided for and taught and ministered to the enjoyment, I should suppose, of His own man. As for the things which are out of this class, they are not fit to be used among us, especially those which on that account indeed are not to be found either with the world, or in the ways of Christ.

Chapter IX.

In short, what patriarch, what prophet, what Levite, or priest, or ruler, or at a later period what apostle, or preacher of the gospel, or bishop, do you ever find the wearer of a crown? I think not even the temple of God itself was crowned; as neither was the ark of the testament, nor the tabernacle of witness, nor the altar, nor the candlestick crowned though certainly, both on that first solemnity of the dedication, and in that second rejoicing for the restoration, crowning would have been most suitable if it were worthy of God. But if these things were figures of us (for we are temples of God, and altars, and lights, and sacred vessels), this too they in figure set forth, that the people of God ought not to be crowned. The reality must always correspond with the image. If, perhaps, you object that

Christ Himself was crowned, to that you will get the brief reply: Be you too crowned, as He was; you have full permission. Yet even that crown of insolent ungodliness was not of any decree of the Jewish people. It was a device of the Roman soldiers, taken from the practice of the world,—a practice which the people of God never allowed either on the occasion of public rejoicing or to gratify innate luxury: so they returned from the Babylonish captivity with timbrels, and flutes, and psalteries, more suitably than with crowns; and after eating and drinking, uncrowned, they rose up to play. Neither would the account of the rejoicing nor the exposure of the luxury have been silent touching the honor or dishonor of the crown. Thus too Isaiah, as he says, "With timbrels, and psalteries, and flutes they drink wine," would have added "with crowns," if this practice had ever had place in the things of God.

Chapter X.

So, when you allege that the ornaments of the heathen deities are found no less with God, with the object of claiming among these for general use the head-crown, you already lay it down for yourself, that we must not have among us, as a thing whose use we are to share with others, what is not to be found in the service of God. Well, what is so unworthy of God indeed as that which is worthy of an idol? But what is so worthy of an idol as that which is also worthy of a dead man? For it is the privilege of the dead also to be thus crowned, as they too straightway become idols, both by their dress and the service of deification, which (deification) is with us a second idolatry. Wanting, then, the sense, it will be theirs to use the thing for which the sense is wanting, just as if in full possession of the sense they wished to abuse it. When there ceases to be any reality in the use, there is no distinction between using and abusing. Who can abuse a thing, when the precipient nature with which he wishes to carry out his purpose is not his to use it? The apostle, moreover, forbids us to abuse, while he would more naturally have taught us not to use, unless on the ground that, where there is no sense for things, there is no wrong use of them. But the whole affair is meaningless, and is, in fact, a dead work so far as concerns the idols; though, without doubt, a living one as respects the demons to whom the religious rite belongs. "The idols of the heathen," says David, "are silver and gold." "They have eyes, and see not; a nose, and smell not; hands, and they will not handle." By means of these organs, indeed, we are to enjoy flowers; but if he declares that those who make idols will be like them, they already are so who use anything after the style of idol adornings. "To the pure all things are pure: so, likewise, all things to the impure are impure;" but nothing is more impure than idols. The substances are themselves as creatures of God without impurity, and in this their native state are free to the use of all; but the ministries to which in their use they are devoted, makes all the difference; for I, too, kill a cock for myself, just as Socrates did for Æsculapius; and if the smell of some place or other offends me, I burn the Arabian product myself, but not with the same ceremony, nor in the same dress, nor with the same pomp, with which it is done to idols. If the creature is defiled by a mere word, as the apostle teaches, "But if anyone say, This is offered in sacrifice to idols, you must not touch it," much more when it is polluted by the dress, and rites, and pomp of what is offered to the gods. Thus the crown also is made out to be an offering to idols; for with this ceremony, and dress, and pomp, it is presented in sacrifice to idols, its originators, to whom its use is specially given over, and chiefly on this account, that what has no place among the things of God may not be admitted into use with us as with others. Wherefore the apostle exclaims, "Flee idolatry:" certainly idolatry whole and entire he means. Reflect on what a thicket it is, and how many thorns lie hid in it. Nothing must be given to an idol, and so nothing must be taken from one. If it is inconsistent with faith to recline in an idol temple, what is it to appear in an idol dress? What communion

have Christ and Belial? Therefore flee from it; for he enjoins us to keep at a distance from idolatry—to have no close dealings with it of any kind. Even an earthly serpent sucks in men at some distance with its breath. Going still further, John says,
"My little children, keep yourselves from idols,"—not now from idolatry, as if from the service of it, but from idols—that is, from any resemblance to them: for it is an unworthy thing that you, the image of the living God, should become the likeness of an idol and a dead man. Thus far we assert, that this attire belongs to idols, both from the history of its origin, and from its use by false religion; on this ground, besides, that while it is not mentioned as connected with the worship of God, it is more and more given over to those in whose antiquities, as well as festivals and services, it is found. In a word, the very doors, the very victims and altars, the very servants and priests, are crowned. You have, in Claudius, the crowns of all the various colleges of priests. We have added also that distinction between things altogether different from each other—things, namely, agreeable, and things contrary to reason—in answer to those who, because there happens to be the use of some things in common, maintain the right of participation in all things. With reference to this part of the subject, therefore, it now remains that the special grounds for wearing crowns should be examined, that while we show these to be foreign, nay, even opposed to our Christian discipline, we may demonstrate that none of them have any plea of reason to support it, on the basis of which this article of dress might be vindicated as one in whose use we can participate, as even some others may whose instances are cast up to us.

Chapter XI.

To begin with the real ground of the military crown, I think we must first inquire whether warfare is proper at all for Christians. What sense is there in discussing the merely accidental, when that on which it rests is to be condemned? Do we believe it lawful for a human oath to be superadded to one divine, for a man to come under promise to another master after Christ, and to abjure father, mother, and all nearest kinsfolk, whom even the law has commanded us to honor and love next to God Himself, to whom the gospel, too, holding them only of less account than Christ, has in like manner rendered honor? Shall it be held lawful to make an occupation of the sword, when the Lord proclaims that he who uses the sword shall perish by the sword? And shall the son of peace take part in the battle when it does not become him even to sue at law? And shall he apply the chain, and the prison, and the torture, and the punishment, who is not the avenger even of his own wrongs? Shall he, forsooth, either keep watch-service for others more than for Christ, or shall he do it on the Lord's day, when he does not even do it for Christ Himself? And shall he keep guard before the temples which he has renounced? And shall he take a meal where the apostle has forbidden him? And shall he diligently protect by night those whom in the day-time he has put to flight by his exorcisms, leaning and resting on the spear the while with which Christ's side was pierced? Shall he carry a flag, too, hostile to Christ? And shall *he* ask a watchword from the emperor who has already received one from God? Shall *he* be disturbed in death by the trumpet of the trumpeter, who expects to be aroused by the angel's trump? And shall the Christian be burned according to camp rule, when he was not permitted to burn incense to an idol, when to him Christ remitted the punishment of fire? Then how many other offences there are involved in the performances of camp offices, which we must hold to involve a transgression of God's law, you may see by a slight survey. The very carrying of the name over from the camp of light to the camp of darkness is a violation of it. Of course, if faith comes later, and finds any preoccupied with military service, their case is different, as in the instance of those whom John used to receive for baptism, and of those most faithful centurions, I mean the centurion whom Christ approves, and the centurion whom

Peter instructs; yet, at the same time, when a man has become a believer, and faith has been sealed, there must be either an immediate abandonment of it, which has been the course with many; or all sorts of quibbling will have to be resorted to in order to avoid offending God, and that is not allowed even outside of military service; or, last of all, for God the fate must be endured which a citizen-faith has been no less ready to accept. Neither does military service hold out escape from punishment of sins, or exemption from martyrdom. Nowhere does the Christian change his character. There is one gospel, and the same Jesus, who will one day deny everyone who denies, and acknowledge everyone who acknowledges God,—who will save, too, the life which has been lost for His sake; but, on the other hand, destroy that which for gain has been saved to His dishonor. With Him the faithful citizen is a soldier, just as the faithful soldier is a citizen. A state of faith admits no plea of necessity; they are under no necessity to sin, whose one necessity is, that they do not sin. For if one is pressed to the offering of sacrifice and the sheer denial of Christ by the necessity of torture or of punishment, yet discipline does not connive even at that necessity; because there is a higher necessity to dread denying and to undergo martyrdom, than to escape from suffering, and to render the homage required. In fact, an excuse of this sort overturns the entire essence of our sacrament, removing even the obstacle to voluntary sins; for it will be possible also to maintain that inclination is a necessity, as involving in it, forsooth, a sort of compulsion. I have, in fact, disposed of this very allegation of necessity with reference to the pleas by which crowns connected with official position are vindicated, in support of which it is in common use, since for this very reason offices must be either refused, that we may not fall into acts of sin, or martyrdoms endured that we may get quit of offices. Touching this primary aspect of the question, as to the unlawfulness even of a military life itself, I shall not add more, that the secondary question may be restored to its place. Indeed, if, putting my strength to the question, I banish from us the military life, I should now to no purpose issue a challenge on the matter of the military crown. Suppose, then, that the military service is lawful, as far as the plea for the crown is concerned.

Chapter XII.

But I first say a word also about the crown itself. This laurel one is sacred to Apollo or Bacchus—to the former as the god of archery, to the latter as the god of triumphs. In like manner Claudius teaches; when he tells us that soldiers are wont too to be wreathed in myrtle. For the myrtle belongs to Venus, the mother of the Æneadæ, the mistress also of the god of war, who, through Ilia and the Romuli is Roman. But I do not believe that Venus is Roman as well as Mars, because of the vexation the concubine gave her. When military service again is crowned with olive, the idolatry has respect to Minerva, who is equally the goddess of arms—but got a crown of the tree referred to, because of the peace she made with Neptune. In these respects, the superstition of the military garland will be everywhere defiled and all-defiling. And it is further defiled, I should think, also in the grounds of it. Lo the yearly public pronouncing of vows, what does that bear on its face to be? It takes place first in the part of the camp where the general's tent is, and then in the temples. In addition to the places, observe the words also: "We vow that you, O Jupiter, will then have an ox with gold-decorated horns." What does the utterance mean? Without a doubt the denial (of Christ). Albeit the Christian says nothing in these places with the mouth, he makes his response by having the crown on his head. The laurel is likewise commanded (to be used) at the distribution of the largess. So you see idolatry is not without its gain, selling, as it does, Christ for pieces of gold, as Judas did for pieces of silver. Will it be "Ye cannot serve God and mammon" to devote your energies to mammon, and to depart from God? Will it be "Render unto Cæsar the things which are Cæsar's, and unto God the things which are God's," not only not to render the human being to God, but even to take the denarius from Cæsar? Is the laurel of the triumph made of leaves, or of corpses? Is it adorned with ribbons, or with tombs? Is it bedewed with ointments, or with the tears of wives and mothers? It may be of some Christians too; for Christ is also among the barbarians. Has not he who has carried (a crown for) this cause on his head, fought even against himself? Another son of service belongs to the royal guards. And indeed crowns are called (Castrenses), as belonging to the camp; *Munificæ* likewise, from the Cæsarean functions they perform. But even then you are still the soldier and the servant of another; and if of two masters, of God and Cæsar: but assuredly then not of Cæsar, when you owe yourself to God, as having higher claims, I should think, even in matters in which both have an interest.

Chapter XIII.

For state reasons, the various orders of the citizens also are crowned with laurel crowns; but the magistrates besides with golden ones, as at Athens, and at Rome. Even to those are preferred the Etruscan. This appellation is given to the crowns which, distinguished by their gems and oak leaves of gold, they put on, with mantles having an embroidery of palm branches, to conduct the chariots containing the images of the gods to the circus. There are also provincial crowns of gold, needing now the larger heads of images instead of those of men. But your orders, and your magistracies, and your very place of meeting, the church, are Christ's. You belong to Him, for you have been enrolled in the books of life. There the blood of the Lord serves for your purple robe, and your broad stripe is His own cross; there the axe is already laid to the trunk of the tree; there is the branch out of the root of Jesse. Never mind the state horses with their crown. Your Lord, when, according to the Scripture, He would enter Jerusalem in triumph, had not even an ass of

His own. These (put their trust) in chariots, and these in horses; but we will seek our help in the name of the Lord our God. From so much as a dwelling in that Babylon of John's Revelation we are called away; much more then from its pomp. The rabble, too, are crowned, at one time because of some great rejoicing for the success of the emperors; at another, on account of some custom belonging to municipal festivals. For luxury strives to make her own every occasion of public gladness. But as for you, you are a foreigner in this world, a citizen of Jerusalem, the city above. Our citizenship, the apostle says, is in heaven. You have your own registers, your own calendar; you have nothing to do with the joys of the world; nay, you are called to the very opposite, for "the world shall rejoice, but ye shall mourn." And I think the Lord affirms, that those who mourn are happy, not those who are crowned.
Marriage, too, decks the bridegroom with its crown; and therefore we will not have heathen brides, lest they seduce us even to the idolatry with which among them marriage is initiated. You have the law from the patriarchs indeed; you have the apostle enjoining people to marry in the Lord. You have a crowning also on the making of a freeman; but *you* have been already ransomed by Christ, and that at a great price. How shall the world manumit the servant of another? Though it seems to be liberty, yet it will come to be found bondage. In the world everything is nominal, and nothing real. For even then, as ransomed by Christ, you were under no bondage to man; and now, though man has given you liberty, you are the servant of Christ. If you think freedom of the world to be real, so that you even seal it with a crown, you have returned to the slavery of man, imagining it to be freedom; you have lost the freedom of Christ, fancying it is slavery. Will there be any dispute as to the cause of crown-wearing, which contests in the games in their turn supply, and which, both as sacred to the gods and in honor of the dead, their own reason at once condemns? It only remains, that the Olympian Jupiter, and the Nemean Hercules, and the wretched little Archemorus, and the hapless Antinous,

should be crowned in a Christian, that he himself may become a spectacle disgusting to behold. We have recounted, as I think, all the various causes of the wearing of the crown, and there is not one which has any place with us: all are foreign to us, unholy, unlawful, having been abjured already once for all in the solemn declaration of the sacrament. For they were of the pomp of the devil and his angels, offices of the world, honors, festivals, popularity huntings, false vows, exhibitions of human servility, empty praises, base glories, and in them all idolatry, even in respect of the origin of the crowns alone, with which they are all wreathed. Claudius will tell us in his preface, indeed, that in the poems of Homer the heaven also is crowned with constellations, and that no doubt by God, no doubt for man; therefore man himself, too, should be crowned by God. But the world crowns brothels, and baths, and bakehouses, and prisons, and schools, and the very amphitheatres, and the chambers where the clothes are stripped from dead gladiators, and the very biers of the dead. How sacred and holy, how venerable and pure is this article of dress, determine not from the heaven of poetry alone, but from the traffickings of the whole world. But indeed a Christian will not even dishonor his own gate with laurel crowns, if so be he knows how many gods the devil has attached to doors; Janus so-called from gate, Limentinus from threshold, Forcus and Carna from leaves and hinges; among the Greeks, too, the Thyræan Apollo, and the evil spirits, the Antelii.

Chapter XIV.

Much less may the Christian put the service of idolatry on his own head—nay, I might have said, upon Christ, since Christ is the Head of the Christian man—(for his head) is as free as even Christ is, under no obligation to wear a covering, not to say a band. But even the head which is bound to have the veil, I mean woman's, as already taken possession of by this very thing, is not open also to a band. She has the burden of her own humility to bear. If she ought not to appear with her head uncovered on account of the angels, much more with a crown on it will she offend those (elders) who perhaps are then wearing crowns above. For what is a crown on the head of a woman, but beauty made seductive, but mark of utter wantonness,—a notable casting away of modesty, a setting temptation on fire? Therefore a woman, taking counsel from the apostles' foresight, will not too elaborately adorn herself, that she may not either be crowned with any exquisite arrangement of her hair. What sort of garland, however, I pray you, did He who is the Head of the man and the glory of the woman, Christ Jesus, the Husband of the church, submit to in behalf of both sexes? Of thorns, I think, and thistles,—a figure of the sins which the soil of the flesh brought forth for us, but which the power of the cross removed, blunting, in its endurance by the head of our Lord, death's every sting. Yes, and besides the figure, there is contumely with ready lip, and dishonor, and infamy, and the ferocity involved in the cruel things which then disfigured and lacerated the temples of the Lord, that you may now be crowned with laurel, and myrtle, and olive, and any famous branch, and which is of more use, with hundred- leaved roses too, culled from the garden of Midas, and with both kinds of lily, and with violets of all sorts, perhaps also with gems and gold, so as even to rival that crown of Christ which He afterwards obtained. For it was after the gall He tasted the honeycomb and He was not greeted as King of Glory in heavenly places till He had been condemned to the cross as King of the Jews, having first been made by the Father for a time a little less than the angels, and so crowned with glory and honor. If for these things, you owe your own head to Him, repay it if you can, such as He presented His for yours; or be not crowned with flowers at all, if you cannot be with thorns, because you may not be with flowers.

Chapter XV.

Keep for God His own property untainted; He will crown it if He choose. Nay, then, He does even choose. He calls us to it. To him who conquers He says, "I will give a crown of life." Be *you*, too, faithful unto death, and fight *you*, too, the good fight, whose crown the apostle feels so justly confident has been laid up for him. The angel also, as he goes forth on a white horse, conquering and to conquer, receives a crown of victory; and another is adorned with an encircling rainbow (as it were in its fair colors)—a celestial meadow. In like manner, the elders sit crowned around, crowned too with a crown of gold, and the Son of Man Himself flashes out above the clouds. If such are the appearances in the vision of the seer, of what sort will be the realities in the actual manifestation? Look at those crowns. Inhale those odors. Why condemn you to a little chaplet, or a twisted headband, the brow which has been destined for a diadem? For Christ Jesus has made us even kings to God and His Father. What have you in common with the flower which is to die? You have a flower in the Branch of Jesse, upon which the grace of the Divine Spirit in all its fullness rested—a flower undefiled, unfading, everlasting, by choosing which the good soldier, too, has got promotion in the heavenly ranks. Blush, ye fellow-soldiers of his, henceforth not to be condemned even by him, but by some soldier of Mithras, who, at his initiation in the gloomy cavern, in the camp, it may well be said, of darkness, when at the sword's point a crown is presented to him, as though in mimicry of martyrdom, and thereupon put upon his head, is admonished to resist and cast it off, and, if you like, transfer it to his shoulder, saying that Mithras is his crown. And thenceforth he is never crowned; and he has that for a mark to show who he is, if anywhere he be subjected to trial in respect of his religion; and he is at once believed to be a soldier of Mithras if he throws the crown away—if he says that in his god he has his crown. Let us take note of the devices of the devil, who is wont to ape some of

God's things with no other design than, by the faithfulness of his servants, to put us to shame, and to condemn us.

Elucidations.

I.

(Usages, p. 94.)

Here a reference to Bunsen's Hippolytus, vol. III., so often referred to in the former volume, will be useful. A slight *metaphrase* will bring out the sense, perhaps, of this most interesting portrait of early Christian usages.

In baptism, we use trine immersion, in honor of the trinal Name, after renouncing the devil and his angels and the pomps and vanities of his kingdom. But this trinal rite is a ceremonial amplification of what is actually commanded. It was heretofore tolerated in some places that communicants should take each one his portion, with his own hand, but now we suffer none to receive this sacrament except at the hand of the minister. By our Lord's own precept and example, it may be received at the hour of ordinary meals, and alike by all the faithful whether men or women, yet we usually do this in our gatherings before daybreak. Offerings are made in honor of our departed friends, on the anniversaries of their deaths, which we esteem their true birthdays, as they are born to a better life. We kneel at other times, but on the Lord's day, and from the Paschal Feast to Pentecost we stand in prayer, nor do we count it lawful to fast on Sundays. We are concerned if even a particle of the wine or bread, made ours, in the Lord's Supper, falls to the ground, by our carelessness. In all the ordinary occasions of life we furrow our foreheads with the sign of the Cross, in which we glory none the less because it is regarded as our shame by the heathen in presence of whom it is a profession of our faith.

He owns there is no Scripture for any of these usages, in which there was an *amplifying* of the precepts of Christ. Let us note there was yet no *superstitious* usage even of this sign of the Cross. It was an act by which, in suffering "shame for Jesus' name," they fortified themselves against betraying the Master. It took the place, be it remembered, of *innumerable* heathen practices, and was a protest against them. It meant—"God forbid that I should glory, save in the Cross." I express no personal opinion as to this observance, but give the explanation which the early Christians would have given. Tertullian touched with Montanism, but not yet withdrawn from Catholic Communion, pleads the common cause of believers.

II.

(Traditions, cap. iv., p. 95.)

The traditions here argued for respect things in their nature indifferent. And as our author asserts the long continuance of such usages to be their chief justification, it is evident that he supposed them common from the Sub-apostolic age. There is nothing here to justify *amplifications* and traditions which, subsequently, came in like a flood to change principles of the Faith once delivered to the Saints. Even in his little plea for Montanistic revelations of some possible novelties, he pre-supposes that *reason* must be subject to Scripture and Apostolic Law. In a word, his own principle of "Prescription" must be honored even in things indifferent; if novel they are not Catholic.

www.ingramcontent.com/pod-product-compliance
Lightning Source LLC
Chambersburg PA
CBHW071014120726
47910CB00004B/1514

9781643730912